NORSE MAGIC

NORSE MAGIC

Spellcrafting with the gods and goddesses of the Nordic traditions

MARIE BRUCE

SIRIUS

DEDICATION
In loving memory of Alexander Gorski
and his Gall-Gaidheal heart. Seeing the northern lights
always reminds me of watching them with you.

IMAGES COURTESY OF SHUTTERSTOCK

SIRIUS

This edition published in 2024 by Sirius Publishing, a division of
Arcturus Publishing Limited,
26/27 Bickels Yard, 151–153 Bermondsey Street,
London SE1 3HA

ISBN: 978-1-3988-4401-8
AD011743UK

Printed in China

CONTENTS

INTRODUCTION

"WE DO NOT FEAR THE LONG SHIPS"

"We do not fear the long ships,
We've seen long ships before.
Men sailed here from the north land,
And hauled their boats ashore."

The Islands, Ralph McTell

NORSE MAGIC—the very words conjure up visions of Viking raiders in their dragon-headed longboats, of trolls lurking amid snowy mountains and fjords, of sylvan elves dressed in green, of the god Thor throwing his hammer only to have it return to him like a boomerang, and, of course, of Odin, hanging from Yggdrasil, the World Tree, in order to discover the power of prophecy and the knowledge of the runes. Much of Norse mythology may seem familiar to us, yet, at the same time, it speaks of an enigmatic realm of enchantment and mystery, whispering to us like a half-forgotten dream.

The word Nordic pertains to the Scandinavian countries of Norway, Denmark, Finland, Sweden, and Iceland. Yet the Viking warriors who invaded other territories, particularly Britain, Ireland, Greenland, Russia and parts of Europe, Canada and North America, left their mark in those regions too, meaning that many countries can lay claim to a Viking heritage.

Wherever the Norsemen travelled they left aspects of their pagan culture behind, from runic carvings made in stone to Viking burials and grave goods. In the UK, we see echoes of their time here in place names, such as Goathland and Whitby in North Yorkshire, or Egilsay, one of the Orkney Islands.

Many of our common everyday words have their root in old Norse, with words such as window, blunder and berserk stemming from the language of the Vikings. As the invaders settled here and assimilated with the indigenous people, they cast their Nordic influence over the areas around them, leaving traces of their magic behind, like the first breath of winter hanging frozen in the air.

In *Norse Magic* we are going to delve into this fascinating chapter of history. Here you will find the gods and goddesses in their dwelling place of Asgard. You will meet the warrior Vikings and Valkyries of Valhalla, the hall of the slain. You can learn to read the runes of Odin and to shelter beneath the cloak of the goddess Freya, as well as discovering the spells and enchantments you need to begin to make your own *seidhr*, the magic of the Norsemen.

From ancient runic charms to the modern day concepts of *vintersaga* and hygge, this book invites you to come in from the cold, to snuggle by the fire and allow your mind to be transported to the wild and wintry land of the Vikings.

May your actions bring honour to your name and your courage never fail in times of adversity.

Serene blessings,
Marie Bruce x

CHAPTER ONE
SEA LORDS AND LONGSHIPS

The year is 793 and all is quiet and calm on the rugged island of Lindisfarne, off the north-east coast of Britain. Known as the Holy Island, Lindisfarne is one of the earliest Christian settlements in the UK, where a group of Irish monks live peacefully, worshipping in the church of St Cuthbert. A brisk wind rolls in from the sea and on the horizon, getting ever closer, is the unmistakable square sail of a Viking longship… the peace is about to be breached.

THE VIKING INVASION of Lindisfarne in 793 was just the beginning and many other raids followed around the coast of Britain, changing the shape of the nation forever. The early Vikings used a smash-and-grab method, burning, looting and killing any who stood in their way. They wanted things that they could trade, so any form of wealth was a target, from gold and jewellery to wool and livestock, even people.

The Vikings participated in the slave trade, capturing people and selling them at trade markets. They were adept at human trafficking and the warning cry that the Vikings were coming would have been enough to make even the bravest heart skip a beat.

This trading of human souls is one of the reasons why the Vikings had such a fearsome reputation, at which we still shudder today. The Norsemen were said to be taller than the early Picts, Celts and Anglo-Saxons and they were also formidable warriors, skilled with sword and axe, so they would have been an intimidating sight to behold.

The stereotypical image of a Viking wearing a horned helmet, however, is actually inaccurate. They would, in fact, have worn much simpler helmets made from iron or toughened leather. They did make use of horns, but these would have been for drinking from, or for sounding commands on the battlefield, rather like blowing a trumpet or bugle. However, much like the stereotype of the witch in a black pointed hat, the horned helmet will forever be associated with the Vikings, despite its inaccuracy.

WHY DID THE VIKINGS INVADE?

The Norsemen were a sea-faring community. The Nordic regions of Norway and Denmark are interspersed with many fjords and lakes, making arable land scarce. In the Gaelic language, *Lochlann* is the word for Norway meaning "land of lochs". *Lochlannach* became the word for Vikings or the Norsemen.

Fishing was a common way of life in the Nordic regions, but those who had no land to till, and didn't want to be fishermen, turned to the seas

to seek their fortune. This situation led to the emergence of marauding and raiding parties, with Norsemen setting sail to seek wealth and opportunities elsewhere. However brutal their invasion might have been, the Vikings were also consummate sailors and intrepid explorers, with a daring sense of adventure and a thirst for travel. They were the great sea lords and pirates of their time. Eventually though, even pirates have to settle down.

THE DANELAW

After that first attack on Lindisfarne in 793, the Vikings made significant inroads in their invasions of Britain, from the late eighth century onwards. By the mid-870s, as the Norsemen had already taken over vast tracts of land in northern and eastern England, it was agreed that those regions would be ruled by the Vikings according to their own laws, known as the Danelaw (or the Danes' law), while Wessex and Wales in the west remained under Anglo-Saxon control.

It is for this reason that so many areas in the north of England have a strong Viking heritage, while in Scotland the Norsemen assimilated with the Celts, thereby generating a new population known as the *Gall-Gaidheal*, a people of mixed Gaelic and Norse ancestry and culture.

Under the Danelaw, people were free to choose whether they wanted to worship the old gods of their indigenous paganism, the Viking Norse gods, or the new Christian god. In this sense, despite their fierce reputation, the Vikings demonstrated a degree of religious tolerance.

Indeed, in other respects, too, Danelaw allowed ordinary people more freedom than they had under Anglo-Saxon rule, which is one of the reasons for its success and longevity. The Danelaw didn't end until the year 954, when Eric Bloodaxe, a famous Viking and then king of Northumbria, was finally driven out of the region. The Viking era in Britain eventually came to an end in 1066, as the Normans ascended.

THE GALL-GAIDHEAL AND THE GALLOWGLASS

When the Vikings invaded the Celtic regions, they quickly assimilated into the indigenous tribes by marrying native women. Often, they would slaughter the local men at the time of invasion, leaving the way clear for them to have their pick of the womenfolk. One can only imagine how distressing this must have been for the bereaved women and children.

The result of this enforced breeding and assimilation was an ethnic group of people who were neither strictly Celt nor Norse, but a mixture of both. These were known as the *Gall-Gaidheal*, meaning the foreign Gaels. They were the original outlanders. Over time the Gall-Gaidheal became a respected part of the Celtic community, merging their Norse heritage into Celtic culture and tradition. We still see this influence in parts of the Highlands of Scotland, Ireland, Yorkshire and Lincolnshire, where old Norse words can be seen in some of the place names in those regions.

While the Gall-Gaidheal were happy to settle in one place and make a living from farming, crofting and trade, there were some among them who craved a more adventurous lifestyle. These men were called the Gallowglass, meaning a foreign soldier.

True to their Viking blood, they were seafaring warriors who would travel as mercenaries in the service of their chief or king. Sometimes known as the sons of death, due to their skill on the battlefield, the Gallowglass played a key role in warfare during the 13th and 14th centuries. In Scotland and Ireland, they were active under the service of both Robert the Bruce, King of Scots, and his brother Edward, who became king of Ireland.

The heritage of the Gall-Gaidheal and the Gallowglass is still evident today with some Scottish and Irish clans claiming direct descent from these formidable warriors. Clans such as MacDonald, McDougall, MacLeod and others can all claim the Gall-Gaidheal and Gallowglass warriors as their ancient ancestors. In this sense, the Gall-Gaidheal still walk among us to this day.

LONGSHIPS AND DRAGON BOATS

The Viking longship has become an iconic vessel of maritime history. These boats, which could be up to 23 metres in length, were intricately carved works of art. The symmetry of the double prow enabled the seamen to make a quick getaway, without having to turn the boat around. A swift exit was essential when you were raiding and plundering coastal villages.

Although there is still so much we don't know about the Vikings, modern archaeologists are discovering new facts all the time, as they excavate long boat burials and study their finds with new technology. Longboats could be powered by wind, via the huge square sail that is synonymous with these ships, or they could be man-powered by the sweat of the oarsmen, who might have been people enslaved by the Vikings. The oars used to move these ships through the water were extremely long and cumbersome. It would have taken a great deal of strength and skill to master them and use them to manoeuvre the ship accurately.

Wealthy Vikings and those of high standing, such as Norse kings and chiefs, would have had their vessels carved with elaborate prowheads, most typically dragons or other mythical beasts. These were thought to protect the ship and her crew from bad luck, sea monsters, and disaster during poor weather conditions. The sight of a dragon ship sailing towards your village meant that you were about to be visited—or possibly raided—by a very important Viking indeed.

Longships were so revered by the Vikings that they would bury their dead in them. They believed that a longship was the fastest way to the afterlife and would offer the newly deceased some protection as they made the crossing from this world to the next. And if burial in a longship wasn't possible, they would instead mark out the grave in stones that were the shape of a boat or ship. Some of these stone ships can still be found in parts of Sweden and Denmark.

As revered as the longships were, the Vikings were not afraid to burn them when the circumstances required it. This was usually because they had chosen to settle in one area, so burning the boat showed that their old life was a thing of the past. Without their boat, they had no means of

escape, so it was a courageous thing to do: a leap of faith. It must have been gut-wrenching to watch everything they knew—their livelihood, their means of escape and adventure, their Nordic heritage and culture—going up in flames, but the Vikings were nothing if not courageous.

These days the burning of longboats is usually symbolic in celebrations of Viking heritage, such as the festival of Up Helly Aa, which takes place in January each year in Lerwick, Shetland.

A BOAT BURNING SPELL FOR A
LOST LOVE OR BEREAVEMENT

Items required: A notepad and pen, a tealight and holder, a lighter, a large bowl of water

Moon phase: Dark moon to release the loss

Write a letter to the person you have lost. Pour your feelings out onto the page, then fold the letter into a paper boat and write the name of your loved one onto the prow. Light the tealight and say:

"As a spark becomes a flame, so I light this candle in Odin's name."

Think of your lost loved one, kiss the boat and hold it to the flame until it catches fire, then set it on the water in the bowl to burn safely as you say:

> *"My love has gone into the west,*
> *Across the water, may they be blessed*
> *I burn the boat that holds my heart*
> *It carries my words to one who did depart*
> *The longship carried my love's soul away*
> *May our hearts be reunited at the end of days."*

Allow the boat to burn, then scatter any ashes to the four winds or on the grave of your loved one. Repeat this spell as often as you need to as you work through your grief, keeping in mind that love never dies.

CHAPTER TWO
NORSE GODS AND OLD MAGIC

SEIDHR AND VÖLVA

Seidhr is the Norse word for magic, while *völva* or *vala* referred to a witch or a psychic of some kind. The word seidhr means a cord or snare, suggesting that the magic would ensnare the object of intention. In Viking culture seidhr was considered to be a female pursuit, largely because witchcraft was ruled over by the goddess Freya (the anglicized spelling of *Freyja*). It was something the women could do to keep their men safe while they were off fighting wars or raiding foreign countries. The word völva could refer to a witch, prophetess, seer or medium—or any women with a strong sense of intuition. Such women were highly respected in Norse society and were called upon to enchant weapons with special powers of invincibility, victory, and so on.

CREATE A NORDIC ALTAR

You might want to set up a special place, such as a Nordic-inspired altar, to work your seidhr enchantments. Use items that remind you of the polar regions or are associated with winter. Lay a white or silver cloth on the surface of your chosen altar, add a pair of white or silver candles, then add items such as crystals of snow quartz, clear quartz, snowflake obsidian, blue lace agate, amber and pale rose quartz.

Embellish your altar with the sparkle of the winter season—glass icicle wands and crystal balls. Frame a photograph of the Northern Lights and hang it above your altar space. Use statues or pictures of Norse gods and goddesses if you have them, as well as images of animals associated with Scandinavia, such as reindeer, elk, polar bears, Arctic foxes and hares, wolves, seals, whales, walruses, puffins, eagles, and so on. Add a piece of deer antler and a set of rune stones and you're all set to make Nordic magic like a true völva.

ASGARD AND THE GODS OF THE NORSEMEN

The Norse pantheon featured some very powerful gods indeed, who lived in a place called Asgard. Each of the major gods had their own realm within Asgard, including one of the famous—Valhalla, the hall of the glorious dead who fell in battle. Deities such as Odin (or Woden) and Thor were so respected and revered that the days of the week still bear the echoes of their names. Over the following pages we look at some of the most popular of the Norse gods. There are many more, so feel free to do your own research into this pantheon.

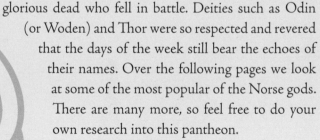

Odin/Woden

Odin is the principal god of the Norse pantheon. In some regions, he is also known by the older names of Woden or Wotan. He is the god of war and death, and the lord of Valhalla. The Vikings who fell in battle went straight to his realm, guided by his nine daughters, known as the Valkyries, where they would feast and fight for eternity. Odin is also a god of prophecy and he gifted the runes to his people. He is the all-seeing one-eyed god of foresight, having sacrificed his eye to gain the wisdom of the runes and omnipotence. Said to be able to transform into an eagle, he is often depicted with ravens—his messengers—and wolves—his warriors. Invoke his aid for scrying, wisdom, prophecy, and foresight.

Thor

Second only to Odin is his son, Thor, the god of thunder, lightning, storms, forests, and strength in adversity. He wields a magical hammer called Mjollnir, which was a symbol of his strength. Made by dwarves, the hammer is said to exact both blessings and retribution. Even today, people still wear the symbol of Thor's hammer for protection and guidance. Greatly revered among the Vikings, who called on his strength and protection, Thor can be invoked for blessings of strength in adversity, victory over an enemy, protection from harm, good fortune, and success.

Freyr

Freyr is the god of kingship, statesmanship, and peace. As the son of the sea god Njörd, Freyr also had dominion over rain and sunshine—and the balance between the two that creates a fertile land, therefore he was a god of fertility as well. As a bringer of good fortune, he is associated with opportunity, lucky breaks, and general happiness. He rides a magnificent golden boar called Gullinbursti. Freyr can be invoked for all types of fertility, whether that be starting a family or a new business venture. He can help to make things grow and prosper.

Baldur

Baldur, sometimes spelt Balder, is the brother of Thor. A very handsome god, he is famed for his good looks and easy charm. A good-natured and benevolent deity, Baldur is associated with peace-making, beauty, splendour, light, gentleness, conviviality, friendship, and good counsel. He is recognized by the golden light that shines all around him, like a full-body halo. Baldur can be invoked in matters of friendship, companionship, happy gatherings, attractiveness, and to help you shine your light out into the world.

Bragi

Bragi is the god of poetry, writing, wisdom, and order of ceremony. In Norse tradition, a poet or writer was called a *skald* and they were highly regarded and respected members of the community. An artistic bard-like god, Bragi composes music and songs, poems, and prose. Frequently depicted with a harp, he presides over artistic expression, creativity, writing pursuits, literature, poetry, composition, recitation, and oratory skills. He can be invoked for all aspects of creativity, public speaking and self-expression.

Hermod

Hermod is the messenger god. Known to be swift-flying, in Norse mythology he is sent on errands by other gods when speed is of the essence. Dressed in a winged helmet and chainmail, his name means war-spirit and he isn't afraid to engage in battle. Hermod carries a magical staff, which he can use as a weapon or a wand. He is associated with speed, courage, boldness, and communication—and can be invoked for all these things.

Tyr

In the Norse pantheon, Tyr is the god of war and bloodshed. He is associated with defence strategy, victory, negotiating treaties, and peace talks, as well as justice and divine retribution. The Vikings would certainly have called upon his aid regularly.

Although he is associated with war and conflict, as a god of justice he could also help with bringing retribution down on any enemy who committed war crimes, or who did not abide by the rules of engagement. The Vikings may have been brutal enemies, but, once they decided to settle, they knew how to negotiate a way forward that suited everyone, such as the Danelaw. Could this be Tyr's influence—and his reputation for wanting a fair fight?

Tyr is also associated with anger and keeping oaths, so he can be invoked whenever you need to confront someone or stand up for yourself.

Loki

Loki is the great trickster—the god of mischief, tricks, jokes, deception, and underhand behaviour. He speaks in riddles and loves to outwit his opponents with his trickery. As a god of deception, he isn't one to take at face value and his word can't be trusted. His tricks range from harmless jokes and jibes, to more meddlesome antics. He is certainly thought of as a troublemaker, so it's probably not a good idea to invoke him. That said, you can certainly learn from his role in the Nordic sagas to help you spot a trickster in your own life…

TIPS TO IDENTIFY A TRICKSTER

In all branches of myth and legend, the trickster will appear. Whether he is the wily fox in fairy tales, or the Lord of Misrule in Paganism, he is always there, hiding in the shadows, watching and listening, gathering just enough information to spring into action and make as much mischief as possible.

In life, the tricksters are the con artists, the scammers, the betrayers, and those who are deceitful by nature. Their motivations are usually base emotions, such as jealousy, vengeance, and spitefulness. Often, we don't even know they are tricksters until the joke is on us. They might be close friends and family members, or trusted partners or colleagues, but we usually don't see their true colours until the trick has been played and by then it's too late.

Unfortunately, tricksters are not a rare breed, so use the following tips to help you to identify any trickster who might be lurking in the shadows of your life and be very careful what you share with them. Forewarned is forearmed.

If you know someone who demonstrates these traits, be very careful because they could be a trickster who is out to get you. They might be after your job, your partner, your promotion. They may simply wish to tear you down to a size and status they find more comfortable to be around. Whatever it may be, watch them closely and be on your guard against their sabotage.

- They use flattery to get your attention.
- They confide their secrets to you to gain your trust.
- They do you a favour you didn't ask for, to set up an obligation for you to respond in kind.
- They may buy you gifts you don't want.
- They are skilled in love-bombing and fake friendship.
- They pretend that they have your best interests at heart.
- They chip away at your time—you can't shake them off.
- They act wounded when you don't trust them.
- They cajole and plead—they won't take no for an answer.
- They speak against you behind your back.

- They act against you in secret, cloak-and-dagger style, then deny it or excuse it when you confront them.
- They like to know the details of your life, so they can use it against you later.
- They draw you close so that they can stab you in the back more easily.
- They speak in riddles, or circulate the conversation so as to confuse you.
- They act as if they are superior and may talk down to you.
- They act indignant when you confront them on their behaviour.
- They try to make you think you're imagining things, or over-reacting. They want you to doubt yourself and your own judgement.

If you know someone who demonstrates these traits, be very careful because they could be a trickster who is out to get you. They might be after your job, your partner, your promotion. They may simply wish to tear you down to a size and status they find more comfortable to be around. Whatever it may be, watch them closely and be on your guard against their sabotage.

DEITIES OF THE WEEK

Some of the Norse gods were associated with the days of the week and we can still hear echoes of their names in certain weekdays:

- **Monday**—Named for Mani, the Norse god of the moon.
- **Tuesday**—Named for Tyr, the god of war.
- **Wednesday**—Named for Woden/Odin, the god of wisdom.
- **Thursday**—Named for Thor, god of thunder.
- **Friday**—Named for Freya, goddess of love and marriage, and also Frigg, the goddess of hearth and home, and domesticity.
- **Saturday**—A day that is associated with Loki.
- **Sunday**—Named for Sol, Norse goddess of the sun.

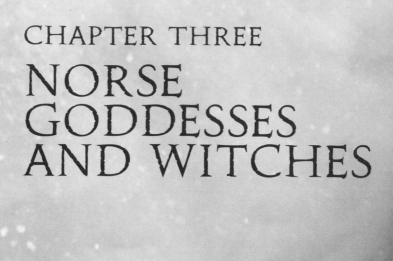

CHAPTER THREE

NORSE GODDESSES AND WITCHES

THE NORSE TRADITION INCLUDES some of the most iconic goddesses in mythology, from Holda and Freya to the more fearsome Norns, who control the fates of all beings. Often closely linked with the practice of magic, these goddesses became associated with witchcraft and are still invoked today by modern witches and Wiccans. Some of the attributes of these deities have morphed into popular fairy tales and nursery rhymes too, such as the Snow Queen, the Snow Maiden, Frau Holle and even Mother Goose. In this chapter we will explore some of the main female deities from the Nordic pantheon.

Frigg

Frigg is the wife of Odin and, as such, she is the Queen of Asgard and the first among all the goddesses. In Norse mythology, she has three biological sons—Baldur, Hodor and Hermod—and many stepchildren, including Thor. Regarded as the Seer of Asgard, she has the gift of second sight, clairvoyance and prophecy.

A clever and powerful völva, Frigg can use her enchanted distaff, spindle and spinning wheel to spin out the *wyrd*, or fate, of both mortals and lesser deities. These magical tools are symbolic of her role as "supreme wife of all wives" and of her domestic skills. She is associated with love, marriage, family, motherhood, fate, destiny, and the magical arts. Call on her for all matters of domesticity, marriage, fertility, and parenting, or to boost your psychic and magical skills.

Freya

Freya, which simply means "lady" in Old Norse, is the seductive goddess of love, beauty, sexual attraction, passion, wealth, and battle. She is usually depicted wearing a cloak made of falcon feathers—the falcon being her totem bird into which she could also shapeshift. As well as a love goddess, she is a war deity too, riding a golden boar into battle.

In Norse mythology, she made a pact with Odin that half the Viking warriors who were killed on the battlefield should be sent to her own realm of Fólkvangr, rather than Valhalla. She is the leader of the Valkyries, gathering up the souls of fallen warriors and guiding them back to her realm and to Valhalla. Like Frigg, Freya is also a völva and practitioner of the magical arts—in fact, she is considered to be the primary völva in the Norse tradition. Invoke her aid for matters of magic, conflict, love, beauty, prosperity, and courage.

Holda

The goddess Holda is a crone goddess and strongly associated with the season of winter. Like many crone goddesses, she can also appear as a beautiful young woman when she chooses to. Attired in a gown of white and silver, she has long silver-blonde hair that flows to her waist.

Holda is the goddess who brings in the winter and she is associated with snowstorms, blizzards, and wild winter weather. In some myths, she is linked to the Wild Hunt—a ghostly procession of spectral hunters through the night sky—though this is more commonly linked to Odin.

She is said to be a protector of children, but, conversely, it was claimed she would take their souls away if they died in infancy, so her name was used as a threat to naughty children for hundreds of years. In this guise, she is often depicted rocking an empty cradle.

Holda is also associated with housework, childcare, and domestic chores. Geese are sacred to her and it is said she could transform into one and fly with the flock. When her feathers fell as she flew, they turned into snowflakes and this is how she became the character of Mother Goose from children's literature.

Other tales, such as the Snow Queen and the Snow Maiden, are also derived from the mythology of Holda. It was thought to bring good luck to thank Mother Holda for the first snowfall of the year and it was traditional to make a wish as the first flakes fell. Invoke Holda for assistance in matters of childcare, for preparing the home for winter, and other household chores. Enjoy the winter snow—it is Holda's gift to the world.

Hel

Hel is the Norse goddess of the underworld, which also bears her name. She is a goddess of darkness and death, but also of rest and rebirth. She is both the end and the beginning. As a deity of death, Hel is incredibly strong. She symbolizes the fact that eventually death will overpower us all. The wolf, being a skilled and merciless predator, is the animal that is sacred to her. As such, wolves are the guardians of Hel's realm in Asgard.

Considered an ambivalent deity, Hel is neither good or evil—she is simply inevitable. Her role is to guide souls into her realm of Hel—a place of deep rest and peace. Far from being a fearsome figure, Hel is said to be an ethereal beauty. However, half of her face is always cast in shadows, symbolizing the mystery of death and the next world. You can invoke Hel for issues to do with aging, shadow work, grief, bereavement, and coming to term with mortality.

Skadi

Another Nordic goddess figure who personifies winter, Skadi is one of the frost giants, who dwells high in the mountains, traversing her territory on skis. She is a hunter deity, skilled with her bow and arrows, quick and quiet of foot, fearless when stalking her prey.

Like most Nordic winter deities, she has dominion over the cold weather and can cause ice, snowstorms, blizzards, avalanches, as well as clear frosty nights. She has a pet wolf called Ruttisdir and is depicted in a cape of frosted cobwebs. As a mountain goddess, she is thought to be the breath of the cold north wind. The mythology of Skadi has also influenced fairy tales such as the Snow Queen.

Skadi is associated with winter sports such as skiing and ice skating, hunting and summiting mountains. She can be invoked for safe travel during the snowy months, the pursuit of winter sports, or for summiting the mountains of life and overcoming challenges.

The Norns

The Norns are a trio of goddesses in the Norse pantheon. Also known as the Three Sisters of Wyrd, their job is to spin out the lifespan of mortals. In this they work closely with Frigg, who conjures up the main fate and destined moments of the individual's life, while the Norns spin out the thread of life to a specific number of years, known as a lifespan. They work together as a team, with each sister performing her own specific task.

- **Urd**—The maiden aspect, who relates to the past and the things that have been. She spins out the flax that creates the thread of life.
- **Verdandi**—The mother aspect, often depicted as being pregnant. She relates to the present moment and that which is current. She measures out the length of thread using her ruler, thereby determining the lifespan.
- **Skuld**—The crone aspect, who relates to the future and that which is yet to come. She holds a huge pair of scissors, for it is she who cuts the thread of life at the point of death.

A SPELL TO DISCOVER YOUR DESTINY

Items required: A silver or gold candle, frankincense incense

Moon phase: New—full moon

This is a good spell to perform when you are at a crossroads in life. If you would like to know what your destined path in life might be, try asking the goddess Frigg for guidance. Sometime after new moon, light a silver or gold candle, and say:

"I dedicate this glittering flame to the goddess Frigg, spinner of destiny and weaver of fate."

Next, close your eyes and consider the paths you have taken through life so far. Try to find the common denominator in jobs, relationships, and friendships. Are you drawn to healing, magic, the arts, or something else? Now light the frankincense incense and draw the smoke towards you with your hand, as you say:

"Goddess Frigg, free the way—your guidance I will hear
Remove all doubt and obstacles to make my path come clear
Lead me with your guiding light through choices I will make,
Take my hand and show the way, as the path of destiny I now take."

Allow the candle and incense to burn down naturally and pay close attention to your dreams and intuition, as you listen out for Frigg's response to your spell.

NORDIC WITCH TRIALS

Although the Nordic regions had a colourful mythology full of goddesses who were inextricably linked with magic, enchantment and seidhr, that fact didn't help the unfortunate women who were accused of witchcraft centuries later. The witch hunts that swept through Europe during the Middle Ages also went as far as Scandinavia.

While witches were hanged in England and America, and burned at the stake in Scotland and Europe, in Scandinavia they were usually executed by decapitation. Following the trial, the accused would be beheaded and the remains would be burned. This was thought to ensure that the witch couldn't somehow resurrect herself or haunt her accusers.

Witch trials took place across Norway, Sweden, Finland, Denmark and Iceland, right up until the 17th and 18th centuries. The last woman to be executed for witchcraft in Norway was Johanne Nilsdatter—a woman who was accused of consorting with demons and causing death by sorcery. She was beheaded in 1695. In Sweden, Anna Eriksdotter was the last person to be executed for witchcraft. After accusations of being in league with the devil and of using magic to rob her former employer of the power of speech, she was beheaded in 1704.

Men were charged with witchcraft and sorcery too. Sveinn Arnason was an Icelandic man who, after being accused of using magic to cause illness, was found guilty and executed—the last person who suffered this fate in Iceland. However, unlike many, Arnason was burned at the stake, rather than beheaded.

CHAPTER FOUR
A LAND OF ICE AND SNOW

Parts of the Nordic regions fall within the Arctic Circle, the most northerly of the five major circles of latitudes, at the centre of which is the North Pole. This far north, conditions are extreme, ranging from temperature to the amount of light such regions receive from the sun. These extremes mean that the Norse people have always had to adapt. Their winters are long and very dark; their summer days last well beyond the stroke of midnight.

POLAR NIGHT AND DAY

The people of Scandinavia experience the phenomenon of the polar night. During the depths of winter, this is when the sun does not rise above the horizon at all and it remains dark all day and all night. How long this phenomenon lasts varies from region to region, but it can be anywhere from a couple of weeks to a couple of months.

While the sun is below the horizon, the Nordic regions experience an ethereal twilight, known as the blue hour, or polar blue, when the area is swathed in a bluish tint. This is caused by the faint light of the sun being reflected by the snow and the sea.

Of course, there are challenges to functioning when there is no daylight at all for weeks on end, but people still have to go to work, take the kids to school, buy groceries, and so on. And yet they have learned to adapt in the northernmost regions, often using this dark time to plan elaborate festivals and parties. Shops, offices, schools, and restaurants place burning candles and shining paper stars in their windows to welcome people in from the cold and the dark. Plus, they make the most of the natural illumination on full moon nights, or when the northern lights are dancing across the sky, often using this time to do outdoor chores and activities. Gathering with friends and family helps to keep spirits up, as they wait for the sun to return.

At midsummer, the whole situation is reversed and during this time, known as polar day, the sun doesn't set at all, giving rise to the phenomenon of the midnight sun. Again, the people have learned to adapt, by hanging blackout blinds at their windows, wearing sleep masks and limiting their activity to scheduled hours so as not to burn themselves out.

Given these extreme and phenomenal weather conditions, which are difficult to endure even in modern times, it isn't *that* surprising that the ancient Vikings and Norsemen ventured further afield in search of more temperate climates.

LUCIA—BRINGER OF LIGHT

The Feast of Lucia, or St Lucy, takes places every year on December 13 and is celebrated throughout Scandinavia. Like many Christian festivals, it has Pagan roots. In the old Julian calendar December 13 was originally considered to be the winter solstice, when people would hold a great feast to brighten up the darkest time of the year.

Later in time, as Christianity became more prominent, the feast became a symbol of Lucia, a Christian girl who refused to marry a Pagan lord on account of her beliefs. She was put to death for her disobedience and martyred as a saint. Her name means light and she was a patron of the poor and needy. The tradition of feasting and celebrating in her name continues to this day.

The celebration involves a young girl dressing up as Lucia, in a long white gown with a red sash, wearing a crown of candles—today, for safety reasons these are often battery-powered. She then leads a procession of women, similarly clad but without crowns, as a symbol of the sun's eventual return. Boys wear white shirts, with white conical hats decorated with stars, as they carry star lanterns or small candles in the procession. This was a form of sympathetic magic, where like attracts like, with the light of the crown and stars drawing back the light of the sun.

Lucia is sometimes depicted riding a reindeer, animals that were considered by the Norse to be the spirits of winter and were sacred to the Sami people. In this sense she demonstrates her victory over the dark season, taming the spirit of winter by riding a reindeer, with her crown of light ablaze.

How to Honour the Light Bringer

The spirit of Lucia embodies both light and dark. She is a figure of deep winter, but she is also symbolic of the return of light. You can honour her in the following ways:

- Place a star-shaped lantern in your window and light it on December 13. Keep it lit each evening until Imbolc on February 1–2, or when the days visibly begin to lengthen.
- Use reindeer-shaped candle holders on your altar.
- Use tealight holders made from naturally shed antler.
- Light candles in Lucia's colors of white and red and ask for her blessing.
- Bake star-shaped cookies or sweet buns spiced with saffron, known as *Lussekatter*.
- Become a *chionophile*—that is, someone who loves winter and snow.

LUCIA SPELL TO END
YOUR OWN POLAR NIGHT

Items required: Twelve tealights, sprigs of evergreen

Moon phase: Full moon, or December 13

We all have dark nights of the soul to endure. Lots of people struggle with daily living costs, unemployment, debts, addictions, and so on. As a patron of the needy and impoverished, Lucia's blessing can be invoked to help with your current situation. First, make a circle from the sprigs of evergreen, then place the 12 tealights on top securely, to represent Lucia's crown of light and hope. Starting with the candle furthest away, light all the wicks, moving in a clockwise direction around the circle. As you light each wick, say:

"Santa Lucia, bringer of light,
Shine on me through my own polar night."

When all the candles are lit, sit in contemplation of your current circumstances and state the issue you've called Lucia to help you with. Pour your heart out to her about your troubles. These could be issues of poverty, domestic problems, home insecurity, debt, or high energy costs. Now end the spell by saying:

"Santa Lucia, I give thanks for your light,
I trust in your aid, help me make all things right,
So mote it be."

Allow the crown of light to burn out naturally. Keep back one sprig of evergreen and press it in a book. Return the other sprigs to nature. Your spell is complete and things should improve for you very soon.

AMID THE FALLING SNOW

Is there anything more thrilling and enchanting than the first fall of snow in the wintertime? As soon as the initial flurry begins, we gaze up in wonder at this cold and magical gift from the sky. Then, a few inches in, we look to the earth to safeguard our footing and ensure we don't slip. Snow is a wonderful lesson in the spiritual mandate "as above, so below," drawing our attention in both directions at once. Those first few snowflakes rarely fail to raise a smile from most of us. Snow evokes all the nostalgia of childhood—snowball fights and building snowmen. It is only the inconvenience it brings that makes us grumble.

Hailing from a region known for its long harsh winters and deep snows, Norse mythology is full of wintry characters. There are several variations of these tales and the names are sometimes spelt differently. In Iceland, Snaerr is the personification of snow. The son of Frosti, or frost, Snaerr had three beautiful daughters—Fonn, Drifa and Mjoll—named for snowdrift, snowfall and powdered snow, respectively.

In Norway, Ullr was the god of snow, while Ymir, the frost giant, was the god of ice. Skadi, whom we met in Chapter Three, was the goddess of winter hunting, skiing, skating—and she is now associated with snow sports, such as snow-boarding and sledding. Norse mythology also features frost giants, who could, in part, be the origins behind the British and European folkloric figure of Jack Frost. To make authentic Norse magic, it helps to get comfortable with winter weather, just as the Norsemen were. Here are some enchanting ways you can embrace the power of ice and snow.

WISH ON FIRST SNOW

Items required: One each of the following crystals: clear quartz, snowy quartz and blue lace agate, a slip of paper and a pen, a small pouch

Moon phase: Any. Perform during the first snowfall of the season

The first snowfall of winter was considered to be extremely magical and powerful. In some parts of the polar north, it is traditional to make a wish on the first snowflake you see—and, if you complete your wish before the snowflake melts away and disappears, it is sure to come true. This spell evokes that tradition. When the snow is falling, take the items outside and place the crystals into the snow. Look up and try to identify a single snowflake, which is much easier to do when the snow is just beginning to fall. Make the wish to the snowflake, then write it down on the piece of paper, so it's tangible. Fold the paper and put it into the pouch, then add the three wintry, snow-blessed crystals as you say:

> *"Snaerr's breath upon the icy air*
> *Brings winter in with frosty flair.*
> *Bless winter's nights with peace and calm*
> *And bring snowflake wishes with this winter's charm.*
> *So mote it be."*

Keep the pouch on your Nordic altar until the wish has manifested. Remember to give thanks to Snaerr for his assistance.

A SNOWY BLESSING

Sometimes all you want to do is acknowledge the beauty and enchantment of snow in a magical way. No tools, no candles—just a simple acknowledgement of nature's winter sparkle. This simple blessing is just the thing. Look up at the falling snow and say the following charm.

"Snowflake stars are raining down,
Holda's feathers fall to the ground.
A blessing full of winter's charm
May the snow do no harm
But light the way for all to see
A new world wrapped in winter's glory!
So mote it be."

SKADI'S FROSTED SPELL
AGAINST SLIPS AND FALLS

Items required: A frosty crystal, such as blue lace agate or iron pyrite, for each member of the family

Moon phase: Full moon

As wonderful as Nordic wintery weather can be, it can also cause many an accident, so to guard yourself against slips, trips, and falls in icy conditions, cast this spell to protect you and your family. Place your chosen crystals on a windowsill where they can soak up the moon's light. Hold your hand over them to charge them with power and say:

"Skadi keep me on my feet whenever my feet meet ice,
Let grace and balance move my limbs when I feel the glide.
Through frost and snow, I'm thrilled to know the beauty
*   of winter's charm*
As I navigate the ice you bring I will not come to harm.
So mote it be."

Place the crystal into the pocket of your winter coat or sportswear to seal the spell and distribute the other crystals among your family members, with instructions that they do the same. This spell is best performed at the start of winter. It can be repeated throughout the year for those who enjoy wintry sports such as skiing, snow-boarding, and ice skating.

Scrying with the Frost Giants

Scrying, which is looking for symbols and images in a reflective surface, is one of the easiest ways to make seidhr with the frost giants. Simply fill a shallow bowl or plain-coloured tea tray with water and leave it outside overnight to freeze. Bring it in the next day and look for images in the surface of the frosted scrying vessel. Use your intuition, or a good dream dictionary to interpret the symbols.

A SPRINKLING OF WINTER MAGIC

Here are a few more ways that you can make magic with the gifts of winter weather, just as a völva would have done.

- ✦ Use an icicle as a temporary wand for a specific spell.
- ✦ Banish something from your life by calling it to mind as you make a snowball, then throwing it as hard and as far as you can. Repeat until you feel cleansed!
- ✦ Write something in the snow that you want to manifest in the spring. Sprinkle the word with birdseed to sow your dreams.
- ✦ Make ice lanterns for outdoor gatherings and spells.
- ✦ For chionophiles like me—make a snowball and keep it at the back of your freezer. At the height of summer when the heat is too much, take it out for a moment as a reminder that the cold, dark, snowy season will return in due course. Put the snowball back in the freezer when you've enjoyed its boost of wintry power. Repeat annually.

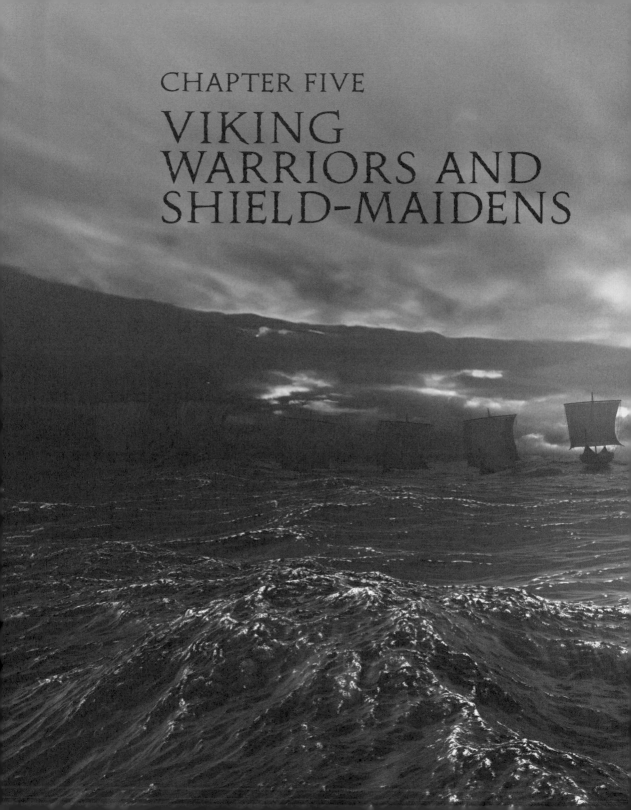

CHAPTER FIVE
VIKING WARRIORS AND SHIELD-MAIDENS

THE VIKINGS WERE FORMIDABLE and fearless warriors. With an average lifespan of less than 50 years, they spent most of their time fighting, invading, bartering, and battling for a better, easier life than the one they had in the polar north. They were, by turns, raiders, traders, adventurers, explorers, seafarers, and settlers, but, above all, they were warriors.

As soon as they had a foothold somewhere, however, they became skilled negotiators and peaceful members of their new community. That said, the sight of a Viking longship heading inland was the stuff of nightmares for those who were about to be invaded.

THE WARRIOR MINDSET

The Vikings had a strong warrior mentality. They believed in what they were doing and they were determined to succeed at it. They may not have enjoyed the bloodshed, but they were prepared to do whatever it took to achieve the results they were aiming for, be that a boat full of spoils that they could trade, or a new home in a foreign land. Simply put, they did what they needed to do to ensure that they were the last ones standing and they didn't shy away from conflict.

This mentality seems to be in complete opposition to the modern way of thinking, where we are taught to avoid conflict at all costs. Yet sometimes

conflict is inevitable and, all too often, people have no idea how to handle it—and so it escalates. It makes sense, then, to develop your own warrior mentality, so that when conflict presents itself, you are ready to face it head on. This isn't about bravado, picking fights or deliberately putting yourself in danger. It is simply an acknowledgement that sometimes the fight will come to you, whether you want it to or not, so you might as well be ready for it. Keep yourself safe and remember that survival is the greatest win. Use the spells in this chapter to give yourself a magical edge as you defeat the opposition and face down any foe. Follow these tips so that you will be the last one standing.

Tips for Dealing with Conflict

- Stand strong, but slightly off-square and to the side. Standing fully square can make you easier to hit. It's also a little too aggressive.

- Stay calm and maintain a low voice when speaking. Don't shout or swear.

- Keep your emotions in check—you can rant or cry in private later when you've won.

- Watch their hands—they could have a concealed weapon.

- Befriend their dog, if they have one, early on in the conflict—this lets the animal know that you are not a threat. It also de-weaponizes the dog.

- Look for a win-win solution.

- When your opponent walks away, stand and watch them go, but not in an obvious manner. Don't turn your back and walk away too—you don't want them to surprise you from behind. Make sure they have left the scene before you continue on your way.

- Get some self-defence training, so that you can protect yourself if needs be.

- Even victory takes its toll, so practice self-care when the battle is won.

VALHALLA AND THE VALKYRIES

The ultimate aim of every Viking warrior was to feast and fight in Odin's realm of Valhalla, the hall of the slain. It was an elite society of men and Valkyries, to which only the finest warriors could gain access. First, they had to die in battle or must have lived a valiant warrior's life. Often, Vikings would pray to Odin and dedicate their missions and battles to him, regarding themselves as his servants. They would also pray to Thor for strength, prowess, and protection on the battlefield.

The Valkyries were the nine daughters and handmaidens of Odin, though they were not afraid to act independently. These swan-winged warrior maidens, led by Freya, swooped down onto the battlefields to claim the souls of fallen soldiers. Their mission was to escort these souls to Valhalla and Fólkvangr, Freya's realm, and train them for the battle that was to come at the world's end. It was also the Valkyries' job to determine which army won the battle. They decided who lived and who died—and they could be prone to favoritism.

The Valkyries are a type of swan maid. With their snowy white wings and sparkling battle armour, they personify the swan's great strength, grace, beauty, and ferocity. As such, swans are sacred to these Norse goddesses. If a warrior stole one of their feathers, the respective Valkyrie would fall in love and protect him. It's said one Valkyrie, Kara, fell in love with a living soldier and used her swan-like song to enchant his enemies and keep him safe—until she was felled by a sword and mortally wounded. You can add swan images and statues to your Nordic altar to represent these Valkyrie maidens of battle and victory.

VALKYRIE SPELL FOR AUTONOMY

Items required: A tealight and holder, matches or lighter, a naturally shed swan feather, or a synthetic white feather from a craft shop, an image or statue of a swan

Moon phase: Full for the strongest power

This is a good spell to cast if you need a little more autonomy and independence in your life. It can also be used to achieve victory in conflict. Light the tealight and concentrate on the image of the swan. Picture a Valkyrie in your mind and see her powers passing through the swan image and into your body. See yourself as a swan-maid Valkyrie, powerful, independent, beautiful, strong, fierce—and free. Now say the following words:

"Valkyries! Guide my steps with swan-like grace,
Freya's beauty in my face,
No captive creature, my spirit is free
By power and strength of Valkyrie!
By Kara's charm I always win,
I defeat all foes with strength from within.
Hail Valkyries! Maidens of Might!
Hail Valkyries! Victory is mine!"

THOR'S SPELL OF STRENGTH
AND PROTECTION

Items required: Two hammers, two white candles and holders, matches or a lighter

Moon phase: Full moon for strongest power

Thor was the god of thunder, storms, and blessings. His symbol is the hammer, due to his own enchanted hammer, Mjollnir, which he used to both bless and punish. This spell can be cast whenever you feel you need a little boost to your personal strength, such as when you have a battle to face, an illness to fight, or a life challenge to come to terms with. Take all the items to your Nordic altar and lay the two hammers across one another in an X shape. Place the candles at the top and bottom of the X, light them and spend a few minutes thinking of the issue you face. Now ask for Thor's strength and protection by saying the following incantation.

"Thor, great god of thunder and storm—
I face a foe/battle in my life, I ask that you keep me calm,
Bestow me with your strength to fight and guide me as I go,
Guard me with your fierce might, keep me safe from harm,
Send a sign you're with me, a blessing with each hammer blow."

Allow the candles to burn down naturally and leave the hammers in place for three days, to seal the spell.

ODIN'S SPELL FOR WISDOM AND STRATEGY

Items required: A black candle and holder, an inscribing tool

Moon phase: New moon to generate new ideas

As the primary god in the Norse pantheon, Odin was the god of wisdom, prophecy and insight. He can be called upon for assistance when you feel like you have tried everything to ease a situation and nothing seems to be working. Invoking his aid via spell-craft means that new ideas will begin to surface in your mind, you will gain deeper wisdom and come up with new strategies that you hadn't thought of before. These ideas will seem like an epiphany when they come to you. That's how you know that Odin has heard your spell and has answered your request for help. Take the items to your altar and think of the issue you are dealing with. Call on Odin by saying these words:

"Odin, mighty god of Asgard, of wisdom and insight,
I call you to my aid this night."

Next carve the rune of wisdom, known as Ansuz, into the wax of the black candle. Place the candle in the holder and say:

"From deepest darkness comes Odin's light,
I light the spark of true insight."

Next carve the rune of wisdom, known as Ansuz, into the wax of the black candle. Place the candle in the holder and say:

"Odin, Odin, hear this plea, grant thy wisdom unto me."

HOW TO NEGOTIATE YOUR OWN DANELAW

Once the Vikings had decided to settle somewhere, it was in everyone's best interests that they should come to terms with their new neighbours. In this, it is likely that they would have taken their inspiration from their

god of treaties, Tyr, invoking his aid in negotiating some kind of equal footing with the native people of the land.

Learning how to compromise and still get what you want is a valuable life skill to acquire. In the Vikings' case, it was a process of give and take. The Vikings understood that they had to contribute to the society they wanted to join, not simply take from it. They also understood that they couldn't have everything their own way. Hence when the treaty was made concerning Danelaw, their right to rule the north of England was respected on the condition that they, in turn, accepted Anglo-Saxon ruling in other areas. Here are some suggestions to help you to negotiate your own version of Danelaw, in any area of your life where a treaty might be needed.

Tips for Strong Negotiations

+ Lead the conversation with what you are offering—don't just seek to take. Bring something valid to the negotiating table early on. For instance, the Vikings offered more freedom to the common people than the Anglo-Saxon's stricter laws.
+ Call upon Tyr and ask for his help in negotiating a win-win result.
+ Try to build a rapport by demonstrating empathy and understanding of the other party's position.
+ Focus on what you have in common, rather than your differences.
+ Define clear boundaries that you can both agree to.
+ Don't view your fellow negotiator as the enemy, but as a potential ally.
+ Don't stick to your guns at the cost of the entire treaty. This situation isn't about personal victory or defeating your opponent. Negotiation is about moving forward in a way that suits you both.
+ Never break your oath, but keep to the agreements you have made.

THE SHIELD-MAIDENS

It wasn't only the men who were battle-hardened warriors. In Norse mythology there are tales of valiant female warriors, known as Shield-Maidens, or *Skjaldmær*, who fought among their male counterparts. They were equal comrades, just as skilled in battle as the men and probably inspired by the Valkyries, who were also regarded as Shield-Maidens.

Perhaps the best known Shield-Maiden is Lagertha, the wife of King Ragnar. After discovering his infidelity, however, she murdered him and took his throne for her own. She was not a woman to mess with.

Over the centuries, the original concept of the fierce Shield-Maiden has been modified, her valour diluted and her courage dismissed. As women became viewed as delicate creatures who needed to be protected and kept at home, so the Shield-Maiden of mythology was similarly confined to her mythological tower, where her only role was to guard the shield of a male warrior. We see this in Arthurian legend, in which Elaine of Astolat guards the shield of Lancelot.

In more recent times, the author J R R Tolkien helped to revive the true concept of the Shield-Maiden, with the character of Éowyn in his *Lord of the Rings* trilogy, and without Shield-Maidens there would almost certainly be no Wonder Woman!

In her original incarnation, the Shield-Maiden was an icon of female strength, courage, wit, strategy, valor, and victory. She was a woman of ferocity and determination, steadfast in achieving her targets, strategic in her battles. Smaller than her male opponents, with half their brute strength, she was set at an automatic disadvantage due to her biology, yet this wasn't enough to stop her fighting for the future she believed in. The Shield-Maidens of Norse mythology should be an inspiration to us all.

A SHIELD-MAIDEN SPELL FOR COURAGE

Items required: A round brooch to represent a shield—a clan brooch is ideal

Moon phase: New moon

Use this simple spell to evoke your inner Shield-Maiden and to live your life with courage and valor. On the night of the new moon, take the brooch and place it somewhere in the moonlight. Look up at the moon and say these words:

"A Shield-Maiden I would be,
Facing each adversary,
I defeat my foes so all can see,
I am blessed by Valkyrie,
I cower not, I do not flee,
I live my life valiantly,
I vanquish every enemy,
From this night forth, so mote it be!"

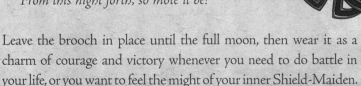

Leave the brooch in place until the full moon, then wear it as a charm of courage and victory whenever you need to do battle in your life, or you want to feel the might of your inner Shield-Maiden.

CHAPTER SIX

FOXFIRE AND WOLF SONG

THE NORSEMEN WERE A SHAMANIC people and they lived in tune with the earth and the seas around them. Similar to the Picts and Celts, the Norse honored the lands of their fathers and they had a totemistic relationship with the wild creatures of the Nordic regions, from wolves and reindeer to eagles, bears, and lynx. They would wear furs, not only for warmth and survival, but to evoke the particular strength and cunning of that animal.

The Vikings also wore amulets fashioned from eagles' feet, wolves' teeth and claws, boar tusks, and so on. While the modern mind recoils from the idea of wearing such things as charms, in ancient times it was common practice among shamanic and totemistic people. In this chapter we will explore how the Vikings may have viewed the natural world around them and used its magic to their own advantage.

THE BERSERKERS

In Old Norse legends, the Berserkers were shamanic Vikings who invoked the spirit of wild, ferocious creatures prior to battle. Often, they would wear the skins of wolves and bears, in an attempt to harness their ferocity, as these animals were associated with Odin and Thor. The Berserkers would fight their enemies in a frenzied attack, with no strategy involved except to kill and maim as many of their enemies as possible.

The Berserkers were no strangers to the "red mist" of anger descending upon them, spurring them on into a trance-like rage. This could have been due to their ingesting hallucinogenic drugs prior to the fight—there are many toxic mushrooms that grow throughout Scandinavia—or it could simply have been a type of battle strategy, used to dramatic effect and designed to put the fear of the gods into their enemy. Whatever caused this shamanic animalistic frenzy, it became the stuff of legends and has passed into modern language as the concept of going "berserk".

THE GREY WOLVES OF BATTLE

Seeing a grey wolf prior to battle in Norse mythology was thought to be good luck and a sign of victory to come. Wolves were associated with both Odin and Thor, so their appearance on a battlefield was interpreted to mean that these gods were offering their protection to the Viking warriors and Shield-Maidens who were about to fight.

As one of the most successful predatory mammals on the planet, wolves are known for working together to ensure the survival of their pack—a fact that would not have gone unnoticed by the Vikings. It would have been one of the attributes the Vikings hoped to invoke by wearing wolf skins into battle, ensuring the survival of the whole army by defeating the enemy.

A VIKING PRAYER TO THE WOLF

As creatures sacred to Odin and Thor, the spirit of the wolf would have been invoked in times of difficulty, when facing adversity of any kind and prior to battle. The prayer below follows that tradition. Use it whenever you need a boost of inner strength to get you through a difficult time in your life.

"Great Wolf, faithful servant of Odin and Thor, grant me your strength and power. Help me find victory and triumph over those who would set themselves against me.

In Odin's name, so mote it be."

THE SIGMA WOLF

Although we often think of wolves as being either alpha or beta within the hierarchy of the pack, there was also a third category—that of the sigma wolf. Although the sigma wolf tends to be male among wolves, in humans they can be male or female.

The sigma wolf, voluntarily withdrew from pack life, becoming a lone wolf instead. While the sigma has all the skills required to work as part of the team, he or she prefers to go it alone. They have the capability to lead or to follow, but they choose to go their own way instead, living by their own rules. Eventually, they may find a mate and start a pack of their own, but they may still withdraw from the new pack from time to time. The sigma wolf prefers to be self-sufficient.

How to Be More of a Sigma Lone Wolf

- Stay true to yourself, regardless of what others might think.
- Don't be afraid to go against the grain.
- Don't always follow the pack—find your own path.
- Stop seeking the approval of others—you don't need it.
- Become self-reliant.
- Learn to love your own company.
- Don't get involved in drama—rise above it.
- Don't compete—as a lone wolf, there is no competition and no hierarchy, either.
- Decide your own destiny!

REINDEER

As the spirits of winter, reindeer were vital to the Nordic people, especially the Sami, who inhabit Lapland and adjacent areas of northern Norway, Sweden, and Finland, as well as the Kola Peninsula of Russia. In the polar regions, the hardy reindeer provided wealth, food, warm clothing, and transport for the Sami, so it was important to honour them accordingly.

Unlike other deer species, both male and female reindeer grow impressive antlers, which they use to scrape the snow away from the lichen that forms the bulk of their diet in winter. These animals were sacred creatures to the Vikings, who often incorporated images of deer in their art. They were symbols of survival through deep winter, of fertility, and regeneration. In some parts of Scandinavia, mythology states that it is a female reindeer who brings back the sun in spring, holding it aloft between her magnificent antlers and thus ending the polar night. To the Norsemen, reindeer antlers symbolized *Yggdrasil*, the tree of life.

FIREFOX AND FOXFIRE

Foxfire or *Revontulet* is the Finnish name for the Northern Lights, or the Aurora Borealis—the phenomenon that occurs when the sun's particles come into contact with the Earth's magnetic field and atmosphere, creating swirling colored light in the sky.

In Finnish legend, the Firefox responsible for the Aurora Borealis has a fluffy brush-tail that twinkles and sparkles with light. He lives deep in the Scandinavian forest, but at night, as he runs around, his tail sweeps the skyline, lighting up the night with ethereal flames, known as Foxfire. The fable suggests that to catch the mythical Firefox would bring wealth and riches for the rest of your days. On nights when the Aurora Borealis is particularly vibrant, it is said that the Firefox is wooing his mate and both their tails have set the sky alight in the thrill of the chase.

THE SOLAR CROSS

The solar cross was a symbol revered by the Vikings, who used it in their art and on weapons. It is a cross with arms of equal length usually depicted within a circle. It represents the equinoxes and solstices, the turning of the wheel of the year, and the inter-connection of all life on Earth. So popular was this symbol that the early Christians adopted it and you can find it in the shops every springtime in the form of hot cross buns. Make your own solar cross for your altar by following the instructions below.

HOW TO MAKE A SOLAR CROSS

Items required: Florist wire, dried cranberries or snowberries if you can find them, two rowan/ash twigs/ other foraged twigs, red thread, glue

Moon phase: Waxing moon

As the moon waxes towards full, take the items to your altar. Place the twigs into an equal-armed cross and secure them with the thread. Next, measure out a length of florist wire long enough to form a circle around the perimeter of the cross. Now thread the dried berries onto the wire and tie it into a circle. Carefully place the circle of berries over the cross so that it forms the perimeter and glue it into place. Allow the glue to dry and use the cross to decorate your sacred space and represent the turning of the year. You can add a loop of ribbon or thread if you want to hang the solar cross on a wall or tree.

CHAPTER SEVEN
IN THE SYLVAN FOREST

APPROXIMATELY HALF OF SCANDINAVIA is covered in rich verdant forest. These woodlands feature both deciduous and coniferous trees, but the majority of such landscape is boreal—which is to say evergreen forests of spruce, pine and fir.

The Norway spruce tree can grow up to 40 metres tall, creating mighty halls of trees and deep dark forests. Left undisturbed, they can live for up to 1,000 years. In winter, ice crystals cling to the flexible boughs, while the tree trunks produce a natural anti-freeze so that they can survive the extreme cold. In the snow, they create an enchanting winter forest that glimmers and sparkles in the available light. Their beauty has made them the stuff of legend, with all kinds of fey creatures, from elves and dwarves, to dragons and trolls, believed to dwell within them.

YGGDRASIL—THE WORLD TREE

Central to Norse mythology was the sacred ash tree, Yggdrasil, also known as the World Tree. The Norse people believed that this tree encompassed all parts of the world, both seen and unseen. Asgard, the realm of the gods, was high up in the tallest branches. Midgard, which roughly equates to the earthly realm, formed the body of the trunk, while the roots were regarded as being an underworld called *Niflheim*, where Hel is located. Other realms branched off from the tree too, including *Alfheim*, the land of the elves, and

Nidavellir, the realm of the dwarves. There were nine realms, in all, that made up the World Tree.

In essence, Yggdrasil represents the cosmos and the idea that all worlds are connected. It could bear all kinds of fruit and nuts, which were said to heal any illness and the tree remained green throughout the year, never losing its leaves. The god Odin hung upside down from the boughs of Yggdrasil for nine days and nights to discover the secret of the runes.

NIDHOGG AND THE EAGLE

In Norse mythology, *Nidhogg*, whose name means malice or envy, was a dragon who lived in the root system of Yggdrasil. He was in a deep feud with the eagle who lived at the very top of Yggdrasil, so he fed on the roots, aiming to fell the tree, in order to bring the eagle down with it. His actions threatened the entire World Tree and all within it.

Nidhogg is a symbol of malice, spite, envy, and sabotage. Unfortunately, you will occasionally encounter the odd Nidhogg in real life—those people who cannot be happy for the success of others and who seek to tear them down instead. Use the following spell to nip their envious malice in the bud.

A SPELL TO GUARD
AGAINST NIDHOGG'S MALICE

Items required: A sticky note, a black pen, a red apple, a knife, a piece of black shoelace or ribbon

Moon phase: Waning moon

If someone is demonstrating envy or malice towards you, write down the nature of their spite on the sticky note, using the black pen. Cut the apple in half horizontally, exposing the star of seeds in the center. Place the sticky note over the star, close the two halves of the apple and secure it with the ribbon. Imagine that you are binding their malice within the apple. Hold the apple in your hands and say this incantation.

"This poison apple binds within
A bitterness and deep chagrin
Malice spiteful, underhand
I draw the line of battle stance
Such venom poisons only thee
Be gone Nidhogg and leave me be!"

Throw the apple away to take the malice away from you, or bury it in a compost heap to rot away the spite it represents. Then be sure to fly higher than ever, like the eagle that you are, safe in the knowledge that no one can bring you down.

ELVES OF ALFHEIM

The elves of Norse mythology were creatures of unparalleled beauty and grace. They could live for hundreds of years and were highly skilled in art, crafts, music, and literature. Their creative gifts earned them the envy of their rivals, the dwarves. (See the charm below for creativity.) In folklore when an elf married a mortal, their children would be known as the *Eldritch*, or half-elf. The god Freyr was overlord and friend to the elves.

ELVEN CHARM FOR CREATIVITY

Items required: A green ribbon, an ash tree, wild birdseed

Moon phase: New moon

This little charm invokes the aid of the elves with matters of creativity and talent. Go to a place where ash trees grow and think about the project you are working on. Say the following incantation, out loud or in your head, as you tie the green ribbon to one of the branches of the tree. Then scatter the seed at the foot of the tree in offering and thanks.

"Elves of ash, beings of light,
I request your aid in this my plight,
Enhance my creativity
That I may craft a thing of beauty,
With Elven skill and Yggdrasil's power
Boost my talent from this hour,
So mote it be."

DWARVES OF NIDAVELLIR

Like the elves, the dwarves were famed in Nordic tales for their great creative skills, though they tended to focus more on making weapons and armour. So valued were the dwarves in their skill, that even the gods of Asgard wanted to carry their weapons, which were often enhanced with magical ability. The most famous, as we've seen, was Thor's hammer, Mjollnir. The dwarves also had a tendency to amass great wealth, hoarding treasure and guarding it against any would-be thief. To this end they are the ones to call on for matters of abundance.

DWARF CHARM FOR PROSPERITY

Items required: Two gold pouches or envelopes, a few threads of saffron, two silver coins

Moon phase: Waxing moon

Lay out the items and spend a few minutes visualizing that you are as rich as the dwarves of Norse mythology. See yourself surrounded by gleaming symbols of wealth and prosperity, an abundance of food, and money in the bank. Next place a silver coin in each pouch and say the following words:

"A coin for thee, a coin for me,
Send me the gift of prosperity."

Add a few threads of saffron to each pouch as you focus on the abundance of the dwarves and bringing it into your own life. Now say:

"Golden saffron, spice of gods, radiate abundant light,
Divine spice of the sun, weave your web of wealth this night,
In love and trust this spell is done,
Bringing with it harm to none."

To end the spell, place one of the pouches in a special place in your home to draw abundance your way, then leave the other at the roots of a tree or in a cave, as an offering to the dwarves.

BATTLING TROLLS

In Norse mythology, the trolls were giant-like creatures who lived in liminal spaces, between one place and another. Bridges, riverbanks and caves were all associated with trolls, who enjoyed causing trouble for those who tried to cross the area they guarded. However, trolls weren't very bright and they could easily be out-smarted. We see a fine example of this in the Norwegian fairy tale of *The Three Billy Goats Gruff*.

In modern language, a troll is someone who is unpleasant to others for no apparent reason. This unpleasantness usually occurs online, though there are trolls in everyday life too. Interestingly, you are more likely to attract the attention of a troll when you are doing well. Just like their Nordic counterparts, real-life trolls try to hinder your progress as you attempt to cross from one phase of your life into another, better, phase. The troll could be a colleague who is resentful of your promotion, or a toxic

friend who is happier when you are down on your luck than they are when you are succeeding. It could even be a partner who is undermining your confidence in your ability to do something that they secretly disapprove of.

Trolls can turn up anywhere and everywhere. So how do you battle them? You don't. They're not worth your time and, because they aren't very clever, they wouldn't even realize that they'd been defeated. The best thing to do is to put them on ice for a while, until they turn their attention elsewhere. Write their unpleasant behaviour on a piece of paper, put the paper in a tub, fill the tub with water, pop the lid on and shove it at the back of the freezer, to freeze their trollish behaviour. Then forget about them—they don't deserve to take up any more space in your mind. Generally speaking, trolls are unhappy, unsuccessful people who hate to see happiness and success in others. Try not to let them get you down, as their envy is usually their own downfall.

CHAPTER EIGHT
RUNIC CHARMS

YGGDRASIL, THE WORLD TREE, is roughly divided into three sections. The branches at the top were Asgard, the trunk was Midgard, and the roots were Niflhiem. When Odin looked down from Asgard one day, he noticed that the Norns, who lived near the Well of Urd in *Midgard*, were busy carving runic symbols onto stones and pieces of wood. Intrigued to know what the symbols meant, he hung upside down from the branches of Yggdrasil and peered into the Well of Urd to get a better look. There he remained, hanging for nine days and nights, determined to discover the secret until finally the dark waters of the well revealed the power and meaning of the runes to him. In the tarot deck, the Hanged Man card refers to this event in Norse mythology.

Although there are lots of different runic alphabets from a range of cultures, the Norse runes are among the oldest. They can be used as divination tools and in spell-craft. In this chapter, we will look at how to make a set of Norse rune stones, also known as the *Elder Futhark*, or Odin's runes, and how to use them in your seidhr rituals.

HOW TO MAKE AND USE RUNE STONES

Items required: Twenty-five pebbles, marker pen, clear varnish, salt, spring water, offering bowl, a pouch to hold the stones

Moon phase: Make on the full moon and use whenever you want guidance

Gather 25 pebbles and bring them to your altar. Pour spring water into the offering bowl and add a little salt. Use this mixture to cleanse each of the stones. Once dry, draw one of the runes opposite on each stone. One stone should be left completely blank. This is known as the Wyrd rune, or the rune of Odin. Varnish all the stones to protect them and let the varnish dry. Put them in the pouch and bless them by holding the pouch and saying:

"Spirits of air, of forest and sky,
Bless these stones of the third eye."

To use the stones, gently shake the bag as you ponder on your question or dilemma, asking for guidance, then draw out three stones and lay them in a row. Read them from left to right as representing past, present and future, using your intuition. The interpretations below will help you with this and offer a starting point to work from.

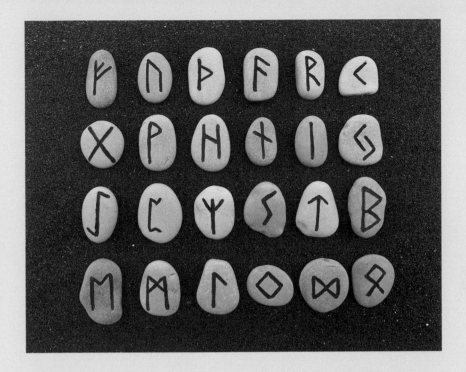

- **Wyrd**—The unknown, darkness, death, an ending of something.
- ᚠ **Fehu**—Abundance, peace and plenty, a sign of joy and happiness to come.
- ᚱ **Raidho**—Travel, an important journey (which could be physical or spiritual), a needed change of scene.
- ᚺ **Hagalaz**—Things will come to a head, completion of something, harmony.
- ᛇ **Eihwaz**—Great strength and resilience, trust, dependability, reliable friends.
- ↑ **Tiwaz**—Leadership, direction, drive, motivation, authority.
- ᛚ **Laguz**—Associated with water, healing powers, renewal, rebirth, regeneration, resurgence, psychic ability.
- ᚢ **Uruz**—Freedom, independence, free spirit, energy, motivation, emancipation, courage, direct action.

- ᚲ **Kenaz**—Vision, creativity, inspired action, applied knowledge.
- ᚾ **Nauthiz**—Associated with need, endurance, survival, bravery, fortitude, stamina, loyalty, commitment.
- ᛈ **Perthro**—Initiation, destiny, precognition, premonition, future-building.
- ᛒ **Berkano**—Fresh starts, new beginnings, regeneration, shedding an old skin.
- ◇ **Ingwaz**—Fertility, family bonds, virtue, common sense, morality, standards, compassion, home life, sustenance.
- ᚦ **Thurisaz**—Great change is coming, be prepared, feather your nest ready to weather the storm.
- ᚷ **Gebo**—Gifts, accolades, achievements, honours, promotions, graduations.
- ᛁ **Isa**—A challenging time to be endured, inner strength, mental clarity
- ᛉ **Algiz**—Defence, warrior spirit, shielding, protection, guardian spirits are watching over you.
- ᛖ **Ehwaz**—A flurry of movement, forward action, teamwork, loyalty, positive change
- ᛞ **Dagaz**—Self-direction, a change of heart or career, forge your own path.
- ᚨ **Ansuz**—Wisdom, communication, public speaking, non-verbal communication, signalling, enthusiasm, manipulation, wordplay.
- ᚹ **Wunjo**—The happy rune, joy, excitement, exuberance, pleasure, comfort, fellowship, friendship, good times ahead.
- ᛃ **Jera**—Things coming to fruition, efforts paying off, abundance, harvest, goals achieved, success.
- ᛋ **Sowilo**—The sun's rune, representing solar energy, step into your power, use it for positive change, know your worth, value yourself.
- ᛗ **Mannaz**—Intelligence, information, skills, adaptability, critical analysis, growth.
- ᛟ **Othala**—Security, stability, increased wealth and comfort, safety, a safe harbour.

CASTING RUNIC SPELLS

Any witch worth her wand knows that carving a candle with magical symbols may double the power of a candle ritual, bringing about faster, more effective manifestation of her magic. You can add runes to your spells to give them a boost of Norse seidhr. Do this by adding runes to petition spells, carving them into candles, and making them into talismans and charms.

The key to using runes magically is to have a basic understanding of the individual runes and their associations. Then you can begin to put them together, combining them into a magical charm that encompasses what it is you are trying to manifest. It's a bit like learning a new alphabet—once you know the letters, you can make words and sentences. Use the list of runes to help you craft your own runic spells. Here are a couple of examples of runic charms to get you started.

A RUNIC CHARM FOR MONEY

Items required: A silver or gold candle, a sharp tool for carving the runes, patchouli oil

Moon phase: Waxing moon

Take the candle and hold it in your hands as you visualize all the ways increased wealth would benefit you. In your mind's eye, picture abundance for yourself and your family members. Holding the image of financial freedom in your mind, begin to carve the following runes down the length of the wax—Fehu (prosperity) and Othala (increased wealth). As you do so say this incantation:

"By power of this runic charm,
I attract more wealth, without harm,
Prosperity now comes to me,
With harm to none, so mote it be."

Finally, anoint the candle with patchouli oil, which helps to draw the money towards you, then set it in a holder, light it and allow it to burn for 30 minutes each day until the candle is gone.

A RUNIC CHARM FOR CAREER SUCCESS

Items required: A notepad and pen, something to represent your career or business, some gold ribbon

Moon phase: Full moon

Sit for a while and consider the direction in which you would like your career to go. Write down how you imagine your plans playing out. Do you want a promotion, a career change, a new qualification or a new business idea? Whatever it is, write it down and dream big!

Imagine all that success coming towards you and that you are feeling comfortable to receive it. Sign and date the notepaper, then draw on the following runes—Laguz (renewal), Ehwaz (forward action), Wunjo (joy), and Fehu (prosperity). Roll the paper into a scroll and tie it with the golden ribbon to symbolize success. Now say these words:

"Scroll which holds a runic spell,
Help me achieve and do well,
This is where I long to be,
Guide me into the future I see.
So mote it be."

Kiss the scroll and tuck it away in a safe place. Feel free to read it every now and then to maintain your motivation to succeed and to keep your dreams alive in your heart and mind. Once your career goal has manifested, burn the scroll, giving thanks to Odin and his magical runes.

A Viking Runic Prayer

Whenever you use the Norse runes, either for divination or in spell-craft, your work will be enhanced if you say this Viking prayer to Odin before you begin. There are many versions of the prayer below, so feel free to use an alternative or write your own.

> *"Hail Odin! God of wisdom and prophecy, grant me the gift of foresight and seidhr. Guide me on the Warrior/Shield-Maiden's path through life and shield me from misfortune. Let my heart be pure, my oath be true and my courage hold strong in adversity."*

CHAPTER NINE
VINTERSAGA

VINTERSAGA is a Swedish word, which translates directly as a winter's tale, but has come to be associated with the idea of a sheltered place out of the cold, where winter fairy tales were often told around the fire. In Sweden, there is a popular song of the same name and even a winter-spiced mulled fruit drink named Vintersaga.

As the Nordic regions can have snow for several months of the year without a break, it makes sense that the Norse people have turned staying home into a fine art. Even when they do venture out into the cold, they are greeted with candlelight in the windows of other houses and ice lanterns along the paths, lending an atmosphere of warmth in the midst of the cold, dark season of winter. This prolonged festive spirit may be one of the reasons that Scandinavians often rank highly in the lists of the happiest people in the world.

ON KEEPING WINTER

In the past, people referred to the practice of "keeping winter," which meant to prepare well, so that you could fully embrace the cold season. In this respect, we can learn a lot from our Norse cousins when it comes to making merry during the darkest months of the year. Far from being miserable at the thought of another polar night to endure, the Norse get festive and start to prepare for the winter well in advance of its arrival, usually during the summer months, making sure that they have a well-stocked wood pile

and plenty of warm clothes, cozy rugs, and comfy blankets to snuggle into when the time comes.

As the polar night falls, they host supper parties for friends and family. They help their neighbors, making sure everyone has what they need to survive the harsh conditions. They go to work on skis, hold northern lights parties in their gardens, and they might enjoy winter activities such as wild skating in the fjords or dog-sledding. In short, they know how to keep winter well, making the most of the glimmering season of snow and limited light.

EMBRACE HYYGE

The concept of *hyyge* has become incredibly popular in recent years—it involves turning your home into a haven of warmth, comfort and coziness for the benefit of your family and friends who come to shelter there. Is there anything nicer than stepping into a warm home after a frosty walk on a winter's day? The sense of safety that greets you as you cross the threshold, the security of a roof over your head and hot food on the table, the serenity of being sheltered from the elements at midwinter—all of these things together give a feeling of hyyge. You have come in from the cold and you are *home*.

TIPS TO MAKE YOUR HOME MORE HYGGE

There are many things that you can do to enhance and create this feeling of hygge. Adopting one or two at home, or adding them into your daily routine, will help to ensure that the long winter nights and colder days are something to be enjoyed rather than endured.

- Light candles as soon as dusk begins to fall, to cast a cozy glow.
- Few things are more depressing than returning to a cold, dark house, so use a timer to ensure a lamp is on to welcome you home after a long day at work.
- Keep fairy lights up until spring.
- Hang a star lantern in your window.
- Place lanterns on your path and doorstep to bring cheer to passers-by.
- Place electric candles in the windows.
- Scent your home with a simmer pot—see page 118.
- Furnish your home with books and read often.
- Play soft, soothing music in the evenings, or learn to play an instrument.
- Have lots of cozy throws and blankets to snuggle into.
- Watch a Scandi-noir thriller on TV.
- Invite friends round and read the runes together by candlelight.
- Make glögg—see page 119.
- Baked spiced gingerbread hearts.
- Learn to knit and make your own cozy socks, mittens, scarves and hats.
- Play board games.
- Make hot chocolate from scratch.
- Burn warming wintery essential oils in a diffuser—cinnamon, nutmeg, cardamom, clove, cedarwood, pine, ginger, eucalyptus, peppermint and tea tree. These will help to purify the air and ward away colds and flu.
- Make hearty soups, stews, and pies.
- Try making your own candles.
- Have a bonfire in your garden and invite friends round to share baked potatoes and toasted marshmallows.

Make a Simmer Pot

Having something warm and wintry simmering on the stove is a great way to scent your entire home, creating a welcoming atmosphere for you and your guests. Furthermore, a simmer pot uses all natural ingredients, so it won't release harmful toxins into the air that way that some candles do.

All you need is a large pan of water, then add the following ingredients; one sliced apple, one sliced orange, a tablespoon of frozen cranberries, two cinnamon sticks, a couple of star anise pods, a teaspoon of nutmeg and a couple of cloves. You can also add a couple of sprigs of fresh pine or spruce that you have foraged from the garden, forest or park. Place the pan on a low heat and simmer to release a symphony of winter scents. Remember to keep topping up the water and don't let the pan boil dry.

How to Make Glögg

In the Nordic regions *glögg* is a traditional winter beverage. It is flavoured with winter spices that, similar to English mulled wine, are said to keep out the cold and warm you up from the inside. Although glögg is usually an alcoholic drink made with wine, this is an alcohol-free version, but you can always swap out the juice for wine if you prefer.

To make glögg, pour a liter of red grape or blackcurrant juice into a large pan, then mull it by adding the following spices—two cinnamon sticks, one sliced orange, two cloves, a pinch of allspice or winter spice, a fresh stem of ginger. Heat it gently on the stove, but don't allow it to boil. To serve, pour into warmed heatproof glasses or cups, and add a few currents and almonds into the beverage. Traditionally, glögg would be served hot, along with gingerbread cookies, or *pepperkaker*, as they are called in Norway (*pepparkakor* in Swedish). Don't forget to say *skol* or *skål*, which is the Norse version of cheers!

JOLABOKAFLOD—A BOOKISH TRADITION

Curling up in a cozy armchair, by a blazing log fire and reading a book is almost a national pastime in Nordic countries. A storytelling region by nature, the Norse still enjoy the familiar comfort of a much-loved novel or re-reading the Norse sagas. So much so, in fact, that they have developed a rather lovely winter tradition that centers around books and reading.

Jolabokoflod, which means the "Christmas book flood," is the Icelandic tradition of giving a new book to loved ones on Christmas Eve. The gift is opened at once and everyone sits around reading their new books, sipping glögg or hot chocolate. Originating during the Second World War when paper was the only thing not subject to rationing, this communal festive reading tradition has since been adopted through all parts of Scandinavia.

Even if you don't celebrate Christmas Eve, you could make jolabokoflod one of your winter solstice traditions—perhaps agreeing with like-minded friends to buy one another witchy books or magical novels. The books don't even have to be brand new—you could turn it into a book exchange, swapping preloved tomes with friends and family members. Or you could embrace the tradition fully and exchange brand new books, with a gift of homemade pepperkaker and a tipple of glögg on the side.

Cultivating a personal library and celebrating the joy of reading is certainly a very hygge thing to do. Books not only furnish a home and shape its personality, they also help to both insulate and sound-proof a building too. So why not put on some soft music, light a few candles, and re-organize your bookshelves as dusk falls tonight? Then find something to read, curl up in a cozy chair, or snuggle under the duvet in the festive spirit of jolabokoflod.

LITTLE SATURDAY

In some parts of Scandinavia, they have another tradition, which they call Little Saturday. This is when people take the time to celebrate the fact that it is the middle of the working week, with only two more work days to go before the weekend. Usually celebrated on a Wednesday, it's considered to be the best night for gentle social activities, which, in turn, increase happiness and help to break up the working week.

Rather than a big night out such as you might enjoy at the weekend, Little Saturday is more about making time for friends in a quiet way—perhaps with a trip to the cinema, or a wine and cheese night with your best friend so that you can have a good gossip. It is about catching up with the people you care about and not allowing work to take over your entire week. It sounds like a tradition that could catch on!

EMBRACE MOMENTS OF FIKA

Fika is the Nordic version of a coffee break, but it so much more than that. It originated in Sweden, but has spread to other parts of Scandinavia. During fika, all work stops and people sit and savour a cup of rich coffee and a sweet treat, such as a piece of cake. They take the time to enjoy a short period of rest. Just as Little Saturday is designed to break up the working week, so fika is meant to break up the working day, allowing time to de-stress and relax. This kind of intentional break is vital to mental health and well-bring, yet many people in other parts of the world are frequently expected to have lunch at their desks, or to work long 12-hour shifts with only a single short break.

Fika turns a coffee break into an event. It can be enjoyed as a gathering with friends or colleagues, or it can be taken alone, in solitude. It is one of the little luxuries of the day. During fika, there are no phones or screens, just quiet contemplation (if alone) or convivial conversation (that isn't work-related) if in company. If you have the three Cs—coffee, cake and conversation, then you have fika. The more fika breaks you can incorporate into your day, the happier and more productive it is thought that you will be. It takes tea and biscuits to a whole new level.

A RUNIC CHARM FOR A HARMONIOUS HOME

Items required: A small pouch, one dried rowan berry for each member of the household, the runes Ingwaz (family bonds), Hagalaz (harmony) and Othala (security) drawn onto a piece of paper and a carnelian crystal

Moon phase: Full moon

Take all the items to the heart of your home, wherever your family spends the most time together. Open the pouch and place the rowan berries inside, one at a time, naming each for a different member of the household. Now fold up the piece of paper featuring the runes and add that too, along with the crystal, which represents the warm heart of the family. Now say the following words:

"Berries of the rowan tree,
Protect and guard my family,
By Nordic rune this spell I make,
By my call, Clan loyalty wakes,
By the warmth of carnelian heart.
We are happy together, protected apart.
So mote it be."

Secure the pouch and place it near the hearth of your home, where it can radiate its own warmth and protection towards your family. You should soon notice a more loving energy radiating through your home and between family members, as they interact kindly and positively with one another. You may also notice a difference in your visitors too, who might comment on the warm, loving atmosphere of your home and may not want to leave.

GIFTS FROM THE VIKINGS

Although when we think of the Vikings and Norsemen, we often call to mind images of unwelcome invaders, pillaging, looting, and sacking villages, that is only one part of their story. The Nordic people have contributed much to the world and certain countries in particular, such as the UK, have been shaped by their influence. Here are just some of the many ways in which the people of Scandinavia, both ancient and modern Vikings, have contributed to global society, from inventions to music and art.

- ✦ Aerosol sprays.
- ✦ Digital mapping.
- ✦ Dynamite.
- ✦ Edvard Munch's The Scream, and other works.
- ✦ Matches.
- ✦ Scandi-noir books and films.
- ✦ Ship-building techniques.
- ✦ Skis.
- ✦ Skype and Bluetooth technology.
- ✦ The battle-axe.
- ✦ The musical catalog of bands such as a-ha and Abba.
- ✦ The Norse sagas.

Far from just being the thugs we remember from school history lessons, the Vikings have helped to create much of the world in which we live. Their influence has lasted for millennia and for that they deserve our utmost respect.

"We do not fear the long ships," for they brought a whole new way of life our way—one that endures to this day.

CONCLUSION
THE SAGA ENDS

I HOPE THAT YOU HAVE ENJOYED reading this book of Norse myth and magic. The Nordic regions have gifted the world with a plethora of mythology, folklore, and legend that is rich in language, poetry, and imagery. They have inspired artists, writers, and musicians for hundreds of years.

The Vikings believed in their magic—seidhr—and in the power of their gods and goddesses. You now have all the information you need to begin making your own seidhr enchantments to improve your life and develop your inner strength and wisdom. Stand strong and tall in the face of adversity. Stay proud in the face of those who may try to humiliate you. Bow down to none. Set your target and don't allow yourself to be blown off course. Negotiate your own Danelaw for a better life. Consult Odin's runes for insight and guidance. Live your life with courage, lead with what you can offer for the greater good of all, and always keep the oaths you make. In short, be more Viking.

May the wind fill the sail of the longship of your life and may we all live to be old and wise, until we meet once more in the realm of Asgard. *Farvæl*, warrior, until our next merry meeting.

Serene blessings,
Marie Bruce x

RESOURCES AND FURTHER READING

TITLES BY THE SAME AUTHOR
Essential Book of Wicca
Essential Book of Celtic Spells
The Book of Spells
Moon Magic Book & Card Deck
Essential Book of Moon Magic
Green Witchcraft
Wicca for Self-Transformation
Celtic Magic Book & Card Deck
The Wiccan Guide to Self-Care
Glamor Magic
Egyptian Book of the Dead Oracle Book & Card Deck
The Book of Moon Magic
Classical Mythology Book & Card Deck

BOOKS ON NORSE MYTHOLOGY
Conway, D J (1990). *Norse Magic*. USA, Llewellyn Publications.
Cotterell, Arthur (1997). *Norse Mythology*. New York, Lorenz Books.
Engh, Svend-Erik (2023). *Danish Folk Tales*. UK, The History Press.
Gaiman, Neil (2017). *Norse Mythology*. UK, Bloomsbury Publishing.
Schorn, Brittany Dr, (2018). *Norse Myths and Tales*. UK, Flame Tree Publishing.
Stefánsson, Hjörleifur Helgi (2020). *Icelandic Folk Tales*. UK, The History Press.
Wiking, Meik (2017). *The Little Book of Lykke*. UK, Penguin Random House.

VIKING-INSPIRED MUSIC
The Wolfstone, Goodall, Medwyn (2021). UK, New World Music.
A Pagan Land, Wychazel (2021). UK, MG Music/New World Music.

BOOKS ON WITCHCRAFT AND MAGIC
Buckland, Raymond (1997). *Buckland's Complete Book of Witchcraft*. USA, Llewellyn Publications.
Cunningham, Scott (1997). *Wicca: A Guide for the Solitary Practitioner*. USA, Llewellyn Publications.

Cunningham, Scott (1997). *Living Wicca: A Further Guide for the Solitary Practitioner*. USA, Llewellyn Publications.

Cunningham, Scott (1997). *The Truth About Witchcraft Today*. USA, Llewellyn Publications.

Curott, Phyllis (1998). Book of Shadows. UK, Piatkus.

Davies, Owen (2017). *The Oxford Illustrated History of Witchcraft & Magic*. UK, Oxford University Press.

De Pulford, Nicola (1999). *Spells & Charms*. UK, Godsfield Press.

Greenleaf, Cerridwen (2018). *The Practical Witch's Spell Book*. UK, Running Press.

Guiley, Rosemary Ellen (1989). *The Encyclopedia of Witches and Witchcraft*. UK, Facts on File LTD.

Horne, Fiona (2000). *Witch: A Magickal Journey—A Guide to Modern Witchcraft*. UK, Thorsons HarperCollins.

Hutton, Ronald (1999). *The Triumph of the Moon: A History of Modern Pagan Witchcraft*. UK, Oxford University Press.

Illes, Judika (2005). *The Element Encyclopedia of Witchcraft*. UK, Element HarperCollins.

Illes, Judika (2004). *The Element Encyclopedia of 5000 Spells*. UK, Element HarperCollins.

Kane, Aurora (2020). *Moon Magic*. UK, Quarto Publishing Group.

Jordan, Michael (1998). *Witches: An Encyclopedia of Paganism and Magic*. UK, Kyle Cathie Limited.

Moorey, Teresa (1999). *Spells & Rituals: A Beginner's Guide*. UK, Hodder & Stoughton.

Moorey, Teresa (1996). *Witchcraft: A Beginner's Guide*. UK, Hodder & Stoughton.

Moorey, Teresa (2000). *Witchcraft: A Complete Guide*. UK, Hodder & Stoughton.

Morningstar, Sally (2001). *The Wicca Pack: Weaving Magic into your Life*. UK, Godsfield Press.

Morningstar, Sally (2003). *The Wiccan Way*. UK, Godsfield Press.

Saxena, Jaya & **Zimmerman**, Jess (2017). *Basic Witches*. USA, Quirk Books.

Van de Car, Nikki (2017). *Practical Magic*. USA, Running Press.